Mediterranean Meal Prep for Beginners #2019

Quick and Easy to Make Mediterranean Diet Recipes for Everyday (30-Day Mediterranean Meal Plan for Beginners)

Dr Marta Kuman

information contained within this document, including, but not limited to, errors, omissions, or inaccuracies.

Table of contents

Introduction

A good diet and smart planning always go hand in hand when it comes to quality food and healthy lifestyle. These days, as there has been a lack of time and organic food products, there has also been a surge in health-oriented diet plans. With so many choices on the plate, it is difficult to pick the best out of the best. Balancing between the nutritional food and the right approach does not come easy. A pre-planned set of rules and guidelines can serve you in the long run. The meal prep Mediterranean diet can be your way forward. The concept interweaved the two different approach into a well-defined structure which can help everyone enjoy good and healthy food with full convenience. Even your busy lifestyle will not become the hurdle in your way, as meal prepping can smartly deal with all the kitchen problems. This book highlights how tactfully you can introduce meal prepping to your lifestyle while following the Mediterranean diet. The first section will deeply analyze the diet itself; then we will investigate the importance of meal prepping. Finally, we will discover ways to subtly adopt this new approach to harness most of its benefits.

Chapter-1: Understanding the Mediterranean Diet

What Is the Mediterranean Diet?

When studied historically the Mediterranean diet can be tied to a specific region or era. But scientifically proven the Mediterranean diet taken a much universally place in human history. Due to its unique approach to food consumption, it brings more balance to our diet and fills our plate with a healthy nutritional meal in a proportionate amount. It is an innate human need to consume food of all sorts, ranging from protein-rich meats to the fiber loaded vegetables, and fruits and the carb filled grains. So, this diet only works in light of such need. Its emphasis more on clean fats and healthy oils for daily consumption. The diet carried its name from its origin, which is rooted in the region around the Mediterranean Sea. People from those places were more reliant on seafood, fresh vegetables, fruits, olive oil, and whole grains. Their approach rightly guided the world to a nutrient-rich meal plan.

The greatest thing about the Mediterranean diet is it does not only guarantee good health, but it comes with so much flavor, aroma, and colors for our platters. Unlike, other restrictive diets, the Mediterranean diet is much more open and flexible. It suggests so many delectable options for every taste palate that it is easy for anyone to adopt. Over the course of time, the Mediterranean diet has significantly evolved according to different regions and culinary cultures. Today, it manages to prevent and cure several life-threatening diseases.

The History of The Mediterranean Diet

The Mediterranean diet that exists today originated from the stretches of Greece and Italy. Different classes of those societies individually contributed to the formation of this diet. There was a great inclination towards the eating of white omega rich meat including all seafood. Along with that, they use to consume lots of vegetables, fruits, and grains in some amount. The typical food patterns of the people in those areas were adopted readily by many due to the diversity of the nutrients the Mediterranean pyramid has provided. Over the years it existed as a culinary tradition, it was not until 1975 when American biologist Ansel keys and Margaret key collaborated to publicize the Mediterranean diet as a health-oriented meal plan. However, its widespread recognition came late in the 1990s. Studies regarding the benefits of this diet were conducted in Madrid and Naples; the objective data obtained revealed significant results. This study confirms the wide-ranging effects of the Mediterranean diet over people's health which were predicted decades ago. Later scientists came up with their different versions of the Mediterranean diet, but the one which was readily adopted was given by Walter Willet and his colleagues in mid-1990s. This approach was closest to the naturally evolved Mediterranean diet. It suggests a similar pattern of food intake as the people from ancient Greece did.

Benefits of The Mediterranean Diet

A healthy diet can do miracles no medicine can guarantee. Mediterranean diet is no less than miraculous if we acknowledge the great benefits it brings to human health. Besides accelerating the rate of metabolism and detoxifying the body from harmful oxidants, this diet can deal with a range of mental and physical ailments including cancer, cardiovascular disorders, and Parkinson, etc.

1. Prevent Alzheimer and Parkinson:

Both Parkinson and Alzheimer are neural disorders which result from the toxic build up in the brain and damage caused by it. The Mediterranean diet has shown unbelievable effects over the patients of Parkinson and Alzheimer, and they all experience improved mental functioning because of this diet plan.

2. Fights Against Cardiovascular Diseases:

All the cardiovascular diseases are linked with high blood cholesterol levels or weakening of the cardiac muscles. With the Mediterranean diet, such threats can be fought due to its good fat content. It does not allow the accumulation of bad fats and toxins in the body while keeping the metabolism active and running all the time.

3. Lowers Bad Cholesterol:

The olive oil based Mediterranean diet is free from all the saturated fats. Resultantly it is low on bad cholesterol. This form of cholesterol is responsible for blocking the blood vessels and causes a high blood cholesterol level.

4. High Life Expectancies:

Good diet and longevity have a very real connection. The better you eat, the healthier you stay. When you eat everything and balance, it can guarantee a long life. This fact is happened to be true for people consuming a Mediterranean diet, and therefore it is prescribed to everyone looking for higher life expectancy.

5. Aids Cancer Treatment:

Another curse of the current age is incurable cancer and the like diseases. Where most of the medicinal and chemical therapies fail to cure the disease, a change in diet have proven miraculous for most of the cancer patients. Mediterranean diet has been proven the most beneficial in this regard. People who are already consuming this diet shows about a sixty percent lesser tendency of developing cancer than the people who don't consume it.

Chapter-2: Why Meal Prep?

There cannot be a one-word answer to this question. Meal prep has so many benefits that they cannot be quantified into a single answer. Our super busy work life has been affecting our health through improper diet. People started relying more on outdoor food than homemade freshly cooked meal due to the lack of time. This has resulted in several health issues from diabetes to high cholesterol and heart ailments. No one can guarantee the goodness of a meal except yourself. Every individual should eat according to his own bodily needs. Therefore, having a homecooked meal has become a necessity for today. In meal prep, you can cook the entire menu for 2 to 3 days ahead, in a day and preserve it in your refrigerator. So, when you don't have the time to cook, like after a busy day at work, you can simply reheat the food and enjoy it with full pleasure.

Chapter-3: The Common Mistakes by Meal Prep Beginners

All the newbies to the Mediterranean diet, make some common mistakes. These are not usually the result of lack of understanding but merely because of the lack of experience. Consistency in this regard can pay well. Here are a few of the mistakes that we should be aware:

1. Lesser Ingredients:

When you comprise on the quality and the ingredients of the meal required, you will not be able to follow up a proper meal plan. Once you are out in the store, it is necessary to get all the required ingredients in your cart. Because if you find not have enough ingredients, there is a chance of missing out a meal from preparation.

2. Cooking an extra meal:

Too less or too much, both are a curse. When you cook more than needed, it will not be consumed in any way since you will be restricted by the routine. Eventually, that extra food will go bad while staying in your refrigerator. Avoid making too much of the food. The quantity can also affect the good quality of the food you are preparing. Cook only as much as you can handle in your set kitchen time.

3. Insufficient jars and containers:

Storage is as essential as cooking the food. If you are not able to store the food in suitably sized jars or containers, it will get spoilt at room temperature. So, it is important to put in some extra bucks to buy yourself some containers for your own comfort and convenience.

4. Having Insufficient freezer Space:

If you are meal prepping you would need enough space in your freezer or refrigerator to stack up all the stored meals. If there is not space, create enough to arrange all the meals for the week.

5. Investing lesser time in meal prepping:

To save your time during the week, you would need to spend extra time on the weekends for meal prepping. Without investing time, nothing can be prepared as planned. It is your health which is at stake here, so take as much time as possible, plan well and then start the cooking.

6. Not labeling the containers:

Once the jars or containers are frozen in the freezer, it gets difficult to recognize the meal. Everything looks similar when it's frosty. Therefore, we all need to label the containers with the name of the meal and the day it must be consumed. It is for our own convenience.

Chapter-4: Tips for A Good Start

To start with a new dietary approach can be a bit overwhelming, especially when you don't have any basic guidelines. Thankfully, now that we have discussed the importance and basics of meal prepping, you must be aware of this concept. What else we all need, especially the beginners are few tips which could give them a kick start until they finally get used to the process of meal prepping. It is true that preparing a meal ahead of time is not rocket science and for everyone, it seems like a simple job. But as we have gone through the commonly made mistakes, we realized that there are certain useful facts which can help everyone in meal prep before any kitchen disaster they might experience.

Few things must be kept in mind all the time, whether your meal prep for Mediterranean diet or you are preparing for any other diet plan. First thing is the order or the structure. When it comes to meal prepping nothing can be random. It must plan and structured as per the person's own routine. The order can vary from individual to individual, but there must be a routine and schedule to follow too. Then comes the shopping and preparing for the meals. We all need a little homework to do before we put on our aprons. This homework includes your personal research on the type of meal you require and grocery shopping according to those needs.

1. Make a schedule and Select a Day:

Meal prepping requires a complete day of planning and cooking. Since you will be preparing food for the rest of the coming days, you would need to spend much in the kitchen on the day of meal prep. So, decide for the day which is available for you. Usually, it is the weekend when most people enjoy their time at home, and they even take pleasure in cooking food. If you can spend Saturday and Sunday for meal prep, then you can prepare food for the entire week ahead. There is yet another way, in which people meal prep on Sundays and Wednesdays, and they break the week in two parts and prepare the meal accordingly. Keep a handy calendar in your kitchen to choose the days.

2. Pick and Choose the meals

From the serving sizes to the quality of the meals and the number of nutrients, every single detail is important about our food. Without choosing the meals smartly, no one can keep track of so many details all at once. That is why the important step is to choose the appropriate meals for the day. Pair a heavy breakfast with light snacks or smoothies in the noon. Similarly, a vegan lunch can be paired with meaty delights for dinner. Remember to keep the balance of both the flavors and the nutrients in your diet. Once you choose, write down all your recent picks in a list.

3. Look for Suitable Jars & Containers:

Appropriate and well-suited storage jars, cans or containers are the true essences of the entire idea of meal prepping. Where to put all that meal you have vested your efforts in? The storage should be over concern because the wrong methods of storing the food will not only spoil it, but it will also mess up with our entire schedule for the rest of the days. The better the storing, the greater the food will taste after reheating. It is suggesting for all the beginners to choose airtight jars or containers which would have airtight compartments, that will keep the food fresh, and it will also maintain the original texture of the meal. Here is the list of the qualities that every container should have for proper meal prepping. A container, having all these properties in one is the most suitable choice for every meal prepper. Such containers are now easily available in the market, and you can even find them online while sitting at home. Go ahead and check if your existing containers match the following list:

- Microwave Safe
- Freezer Safe
- Reusable
- Dishwasher Safe
- BPA Free
- Stackable

The microwavable jar makes it easy to reheat the food any time you want. Transferring from one container to another for reheating is messy and should be avoided as you can't waste much time on it.

A freezer safe container retains its shape even at extremely low temperatures. Sometimes the food expands due to the freezing of the liquid, and it can affect the container they are preserved. A freezer safe container will bear all such effects without deforming in any way.

Easy to wash and reusable containers are most needed for meal prep. It is obvious that you will need lots of containers whenever your meal prep, so you cannot simply stack up hundreds of containers in your kitchen. Buy some long-lasting, durable and high-quality containers to use again and again. These jars must be dishwasher safe to make their handling and washing easier and convenient.

Lastly, the containers must be stackable. Since you will be preparing lots of meal ahead, your refrigerator or freezer will get flooded with the packed food. The stackable containers take a lesser room and can be adjusted in any arrangement inside the fridge. The multi-layered long or wide containers can be quite useful in this regard. Keep the meal of a single day in a single container with separate compartments. It will also save you from excessive labeling.

4. Jot It down:

Whatever you plan or prepare, writing or jotting it down somewhere is as necessary as the planning itself. Several people count on their memory to recognize the meal for the specific day. As the days go by, they tend to forget the entire plan and mess up with the schedule. Meals get mixed up or confused which results in one big confusion overall. To avoid that mess even before happening, it better to write it down while you label the food according to the days. In fact, create the list as per the labels of the containers. It is not always necessary to paper write everything, make notes somewhere on your cellphone if you are a tech-friendly individual. But keep it safe until the next session of meal prepping. You can use the same pattern repeatedly or alternating one-week plan with the other to create variations. By writing it down, it can all be handled easily without much confusion.

5. Keep Up the Routine:

Following the routine is most important in meal prep. If you have planned several meals of the week and yet fail to follow the schedule or keep up the routine, all your efforts will go in vain. By messing up with the schedule, you will mess up the entire menu. Moreover, you will also lose track of nutrients and caloric content. To maintain the complete balance, it therefore important to stick to the routine and schedule. Keep the written list always with you, or display it somewhere in your kitchen so that it would constantly remind of all the meals for the day.

Chapter-5: 30-Day Meal Plan

It is necessary to make a meal plan if you are planning to follow the Mediterranean diet. These recipes are tasty to eat and easy to cook for the individuals who seriously want to follow the Mediterranean diet. The 30 Days Meal Plan for the Mediterranean Diet is as follows with the delicious breakfast, lunch and dinner recipes. This is a complete 30 days meal plan along with the delicious and mouthwatering recipes listed below.

Day 1
Breakfast: Mediterranean Smoothie
Lunch: Napoletana Hoki Soup
Dinner: Sauce Dipped Mussels

Day 2
Breakfast: Green Poached Egg Toasts
Lunch: Black Beans Feta Salad
Dinner: Mediterranean Chicken with Potatoes

Day 3
Breakfast: Spinach Parmesan Baked Eggs
Lunch: Loaded Mediterranean Veggie Sandwich
Dinner: Lamb Pasta and Cheese

Day 4
Breakfast: Soufflé Omelet with Mushrooms
Lunch: Red Barley Soup
Dinner: Lobster Rice Paella

Day 5
Breakfast: Pina Colada Smoothie
Lunch: Aubergine and Pepper Salad
Dinner: Chicken with Tomato Sauce

Day 6

Breakfast: Sweet Potato Breakfast Hash
Lunch: Pita Sandwich
Dinner: Mediterranean Beef Pinwheels

Day 7

Breakfast: Spinach and Feta Baked Egg
Lunch: Passata Cream Soup
Dinner: Seafood with Couscous Salad

Day 8

Breakfast: Kiwi Smoothie
Lunch: Mediterranean Sardine Salad
Dinner: Roasted Mediterranean Chicken

Day 9

Breakfast: Mediterranean Smoothie
Lunch: Charred Green Beans with Mustard
Dinner: Garlic and Rosemary Mediterranean Pork Roast

Day 10

Breakfast: Green Poached Egg Toasts
Lunch: Lemony Mushroom and Herb Rice
Dinner: Mixed Seafood Stew

Day 11

Breakfast: Spinach Parmesan Baked Eggs
Lunch: Smoky Roasted Vegetables
Dinner: Hasselback Caprese Chicken

Day 12

Breakfast: Soufflé Omelet with Mushrooms
Lunch: Cashew and Bell Pepper Rice

Dinner: Vegetables Lamb Shanks

Day 13
Breakfast: Pina Colada Smoothie
Lunch: Roasted Vegetable Tabbouleh
Dinner: Seafood Garlic Couscous

Day 14
Breakfast: Sweet Potato Breakfast Hash
Lunch: Moroccan Couscous
Dinner: Olive Chicken

Day 15
Breakfast: Spinach and Feta Baked Egg
Lunch: Parmesan Roasted Broccoli
Dinner: Mediterranean Beef Kofta

Day 16
Breakfast: Mediterranean Smoothie
Lunch: Spinach Beans
Dinner: Fish and Vegetable Parcels

Day 17
Breakfast: Green Poached Egg Toasts
Lunch: Napoletana Hoki Soup
Dinner: Mediterranean Chicken and Orzo

Day 18
Breakfast: Spinach Parmesan Baked Eggs
Lunch: Black Beans Feta Salad
Dinner: Blue-Cheese Topped Pork Chops

Day 19

Breakfast: Soufflé Omelet with Mushrooms
Lunch: Loaded Mediterranean Veggie Sandwich
Dinner: Saffron Fish Gratins

Day 20
Breakfast: Pina Colada Smoothie
Lunch: Red Barley Soup
Dinner: Lemon-Thyme Chicken

Day 21
Breakfast: Sweet Potato Breakfast Hash
Lunch: Aubergine and Pepper Salad
Dinner: Baked Lamb Tray

Day 22
Breakfast: Bacon Bok Choy Samba
Lunch: Pita Sandwich
Dinner: Crusty Grilled Clams

Day 23
Breakfast: Spinach and Feta Baked Egg
Lunch: Passata Cream Soup
Dinner: Mediterranean Chicken Quinoa Bowl

Day 24
Breakfast: Mediterranean Smoothie
Lunch: Mediterranean Sardine Salad
Dinner: Greek Beef Steak and Hummus Plate

Day 25
Breakfast: Green Poached Egg Toasts
Lunch: Charred Green Beans with Mustard
Dinner: Sauce Dipped Mussels

Day 26

Breakfast: Spinach Parmesan Baked Eggs
Lunch: Lemony Mushroom and Herb Rice
Dinner: Mediterranean Chicken with Potatoes

Day 27

Breakfast: Soufflé Omelet with Mushrooms
Lunch: Smoky Roasted Vegetables
Dinner: Lamb Pasta and Cheese

Day 28

Breakfast: Pina Colada Smoothie
Lunch: Cashew and Bell Pepper Rice
Dinner: Lobster Rice Paella

Day 29

Breakfast: Sweet Potato Breakfast Hash
Lunch: Moroccan Couscous
Dinner: Olive Chicken

Day 30

Breakfast: Spinach and Feta Baked Egg
Lunch: Parmesan Roasted Broccoli
Dinner: Garlic and Rosemary Mediterranean Pork Roast

Chapter-6: Breakfast Recipes

Mediterranean Smoothie

Preparation Time: 10 minutes
Servings: 2

Ingredients:

- 4 cups baby spinach, loosely packed
- 12 ice cubes
- 1 cup coconut milk
- 2 teaspoons fresh ginger root, minced
- 2 frozen bananas
- 1 cup beet juice
- 2 small mangoes
- 2 teaspoons fresh ginger root, minced
- 2 frozen bananas
- 1 cup beet juice
- 2 small mangoes

Method:

1. Put all the ingredients in a blender and blend until smooth.
2. Pour into 2 glasses and immediately serve.

Nutritional Value:

- Calories 528
- Total Fat 1.7 g
- Saturated Fat 0.4 g
- Cholesterol 2 mg
- Total Carbs 125.5 g
- Dietary Fiber 18.5 g
- Sugar 84.9 g
- Protein 13.1 g

Green Poached Egg Toasts

Preparation Time: 15 minutes
Servings: 4

Ingredients:

- 4 bread slices, toasted
- 2 teaspoons soy sauce
- Salt and black pepper, to taste
- 4 oz avocado flesh, mashed
- ½ teaspoon lemon juice
- 7 oz smoked salmon
- 4 eggs

Method:

1. Boil water in a pot and generate a whirlpool in it.
2. Snap 2 eggs in it and let it cook.
3. Repeat the same procedure with the other 2 eggs.
4. Transfer all the eggs immediately to an ice bath for 10 seconds.
5. Scoop out the fresh avocado flesh into a bowl and mash well.
6. Place 4 toasted slices in the serving plates and spread the avocado mash generously over them.
7. Divide the smoked salmon over the bread slices.
8. Drizzle half of the soy sauce, lemon juice, salt and black pepper over each of the toasts.
9. Top each with one poached egg and serve immediately.

Nutritional Value:

- Calories 195
- Total Fat 11.2 g
- Saturated Fat 2.5 g
- Cholesterol 175 mg
- Total Carbs 7.8 g
- Dietary Fiber 2.3 g
- Sugar 1 g
- Protein 16.1 g

Spinach Parmesan Baked Eggs

Preparation Time: 25 minutes
Servings: 2

Ingredients:

- ¼ cup fat-free parmesan cheese, grated
- 1 garlic clove, minced
- ½ small tomato, diced small
- 1 teaspoon olive oil
- 2 eggs
- 2 cups baby spinach

Method:

1. Preheat the oven to 360 degrees F and grease an 8-inch casserole dish.
2. Put olive oil in a large skillet over medium heat and stir in garlic and spinach.
3. Sauté for about 3 minutes and completely drain.
4. Add parmesan cheese and transfer this mixture to the casserole dish.
5. Make two wells in the spinach mixture and crack one egg into each well.
6. Place the casserole dish in the oven and bake for about 15 minutes.
7. Remove from the oven and serve warm.

Nutritional Value:

- Calories 231
- Total Fat 15.9 g
- Saturated Fat 7.7 g
- Cholesterol 194 mg
- Total Carbs 4.3 g
- Dietary Fiber 1 g
- Sugar 1.1 g
- Protein 20.2 g

Soufflé Omelet with Mushrooms

Preparation Time: 25 minutes
Servings: 3

Ingredients:

- ½ tablespoon parsley, minced
- 1 garlic clove, minced
- ¼ teaspoon salt
- ½ teaspoon extra-virgin olive oil
- 4 ounces mushrooms, sliced
- ¼ teaspoon black pepper
- 1/8 cup cheddar cheese, grated
- 2 small eggs, separated

Method:
1. Heat oil in a non-stick skillet over medium-high heat and add garlic.
2. Sauté for about 1 minute and stir in the mushrooms.
3. Cook for about 10 minutes and sprinkle parsley on top.
4. Beat egg yolks in a bowl and whisk the egg whites separately.
5. Season this mixture with salt, black pepper and top with cheddar cheese.
6. Heat a large skillet and pour in the egg batter.
7. Cover the lid and spread mushrooms over one side of the egg.
8. Fold it over the mushrooms and dish out to serve warm.

Nutritional Value:
- Calories 142
- Total Fat 9.9 g
- Saturated Fat 3.8 g
- Cholesterol 196 mg
- Total Carbs 3.6 g
- Dietary Fiber 0.9 g
- Sugar 1.8 g
- Protein 11.2 g

Pina Colada Smoothie

Preparation Time: 10 minutes
Servings: 4

Ingredients:

- 4 bananas
- 2 cups pineapple, peeled and sliced
- 2 cups mangoes, cored and diced
- 1 cup ice
- 4 tablespoons flaxseed
- 1¼ cups coconut milk

Method:

1. Put all the ingredients in a blender and blend until smooth.
2. Pour into 4 glasses and immediately serve.

Nutritional Value:

- Calories 417
- Total Fat 22.1 g
- Saturated Fat 17.4 g
- Cholesterol 0 mg
- Total Carbs 56.6 g
- Dietary Fiber 9.2 g
- Sugar 36.6 g
- Protein 5.5 g

Sweet Potato Breakfast Hash

Preparation Time: 30 minutes
Servings: 3

Ingredients:

- ¼ teaspoon ground white pepper
- ¼ teaspoon salt
- ½ teaspoon honey
- ½ tablespoon lemon juice
- ½ avocado, peeled, pit removed, and diced
- 1½ tablespoons olive oil
- 1 garlic clove, minced
- 1 sweet potato, peeled and cubed
- ½ tablespoon apple cider vinegar
- 1/8 cup yellow onion, diced
- 4 ounces low sodium ham, diced
- 1/8 cup green bell pepper, diced

Method:

1. Preheat the oven to 440 degrees F and lightly grease a baking sheet.
2. Season the sweet potatoes with black pepper and salt, and drizzle with a half tablespoon of olive oil.
3. Arrange these seasoned potatoes on the baking sheet and transfer in the oven.
4. Bake for about 14 minutes and remove from the oven.
5. Combine honey, apple cider vinegar, 1 tablespoon olive oil and garlic in a bowl.
6. Heat the skillet and add remaining olive oil, bell pepper and onions in it.
7. Sauté until soft and add baked potatoes and ham.
8. Cook until the meat turns golden and turn off the heat.
9. Season the mixture with vinegar sauce, lemon juice and avocado.
10. Dish out in a serving platter and serve warm.

Nutritional Value:

- Calories 382
- Total Fat 23.4 g
- Saturated Fat 5.7 g
- Cholesterol 65 mg

- Total Carbs 23.4 g
- Dietary Fiber 6 g
- Sugar 1.9 g
- Protein 20.4 g

Spinach and Feta Baked Egg

Preparation Time: 25 minutes
Servings: 2

Ingredients:

- ½ cup cooked spinach, squeezed
- ¼ cup fat-free feta cheese
- 2 eggs

Method:

1. Preheat the oven to 365 degrees F and grease a muffin pan with muffin cups.
2. Divide the spinach into 2 muffin cups and press gently into the bottom.
3. Stir in the whisked eggs and top with feta cheese.
4. Bake for about 15 minutes and dish out in serving plates to serve warm.

Nutritional Value:

- Calories 114
- Total Fat 8.4 g
- Saturated Fat 4.2 g
- Cholesterol 180 mg
- Total Carbs 1.4 g
- Dietary Fiber 0.2 g
- Sugar 1.1 g
- Protein 8.4 g

Kiwi Smoothie

Preparation Time: 10 minutes
Servings: 2

Ingredients:

- 1 cup basil leaves
- 2 bananas
- 1 cup fresh pineapple
- 10 kiwis

Method:

1. Put all the ingredients in a blender and blend until smooth.
2. Pour into 2 glasses and immediately serve.

Nutritional Value:

- Calories 378
- Total Fat 2.5 g
- Saturated Fat 0.3 g
- Cholesterol 0 mg
- Total Carbs 93.5 g
- Dietary Fiber 15.6 g
- Sugar 56.7 g
- Protein 6.1 g

Chapter-7: Soups, Salads and Sandwiches

Napoletana Hoki Soup

Preparation Time: 30 minutes
Servings: 2

Ingredients:

- ½ bulb fennel, finely sliced
- 1 cup fish stock
- ¼ cup basil leaves, torn
- 2½ tablespoons half-fat crème Fraiche, to serve
- 1 zucchini, finely sliced
- ½ teaspoon chipotle chili in adobo sauce or chili paste, to serve
- ½ pound Napoletana pasta sauce
- ½ pound hoki fillet, defrosted

Method:

1. Boil pasta sauce and stock in a large cooking pan.
2. Let it simmer for about 4 minutes and stir in the fennel and zucchinis.
3. Cook for about 3 minutes and add the hoki fillets.
4. Cook for about 4 minutes on low heat and fish stock and basil.
5. Mix crème Fraiche with chili paste and Napoletana pasta sauce in a small bowl.
6. Garnish the soup with this seasoned crème Fraiche and serve.

Nutritional Value:

- Calories 459
- Total Fat 21.8 g
- Saturated Fat 3.7 g
- Cholesterol 17 mg
- Total Carbs 44.5 g
- Dietary Fiber 5.7 g
- Sugar 7.5 g
- Protein 18.6 g

Black Beans Feta Salad

Preparation Time: 25 minutes
Servings: 8

Ingredients:

- 8 Roma tomatoes, chopped
- 4 (14.5 ounce) cans black beans, drained
- 1 red onion, sliced
- 2 lemons, juiced
- Salt, to taste
- ½ cup feta cheese, crumbled
- 4 tablespoons olive oil
- ½ cup fresh dill, chopped

Method:

1. Put all the ingredients in a bowl except feta cheese and salt.
2. Top the beans salad with feta cheese and salt to immediately serve.

Nutritional Value:

- Calories 362
- Total Fat 19.8 g
- Saturated Fat 4.9 g
- Cholesterol 17 mg
- Total Carbs 38.2 g
- Dietary Fiber 11.1 g
- Sugar 12.8 g
- Protein 14.1 g

Loaded Mediterranean Veggie Sandwich

Preparation Time: 25 minutes
Servings: 2

Ingredients:

- ¼ cup sprouts
- 3 tablespoons cilantro jalapeno hummus
- 2 slices whole wheat bread
- 1 whole leaf fresh lettuce
- 1 red onion, thinly sliced
- 2 whole cucumbers, thinly sliced
- 2 whole tomatoes, thinly sliced
- 2 Peppadew peppers, chopped
- 2 tablespoons feta cheese, crumbled

Method:

1. Toast the bread slices and spread hummus on both the sides of slices.
2. Layer with sprouts, tomato, feta cheese, lettuce, red onion, cucumber and peppadew peppers.
3. Slice the sandwich and immediately serve.

Nutritional Value:

- Calories 248
- Total Fat 5.2 g
- Saturated Fat 1.7 g
- Cholesterol 8 mg
- Total Carbs 40.3 g
- Dietary Fiber 7.3 g
- Sugar 17.4 g
- Protein 9.9 g

Red Barley Soup

Preparation Time: 1 hour 10 minutes
Servings: 8

Ingredients:

- 4 small onions, diced
- 14 cups water
- 6 tablespoons red wine
- 1-pound small red lentils, dried
- 12 garlic cloves
- 4 teaspoons smoked paprika
- Cheddar cheese, to serve
- 1 cup barley
- 2 celery stalks
- 4 bay leaves
- 2 teaspoons salt
- Brown bread cubes, to serve
- 1 cup olive oil
- 4 medium carrots, diced
- 3 cups tomato sauce
- 2 tablespoons dried Greek oregano
- Black pepper, to taste

Method:

1. Put the lentils and water in a cooking pot and boil for about 5 minutes.
2. Stir in barley along with rest of the ingredients and 12 cups of water.
3. Cover and cook for about 45 minutes until it thickens.
4. Eliminate the bay leaves and top with cheddar cheese to serve.

Nutritional Value:

- Calories 470
- Total Fat 26.9 g
- Saturated Fat 3.8 g
- Cholesterol 0 mg

- Total Carbs 51.5 g
- Dietary Fiber 13.2 g
- Sugar 18 g
- Protein 11.8 g

Aubergine and Pepper Salad

Preparation Time: 40 minutes
Servings: 8

Ingredients:

- 1¼ cups ready-roasted red pepper, soaked and drained
- 3 aubergines
- 2 tablespoons olive oil
- ¼ cup thyme leaves
- 2 garlic cloves, sliced
- Salt and black pepper, to taste

Method:

1. Preheat the oven to 330 degrees F and grease a baking tray.
2. Set the griddle pan over high heat and pour in oil and aubergines.
3. Cook for about 3 minutes on each side until grilled.
4. Add the grilled aubergines and ready-roasted red peppers to a baking tray.
5. Drizzle with olive oil and top with thyme leaves, garlic slices, salt and black pepper.
6. Transfer the baking tray in the oven and bake for about 30 minutes.
7. Dish out in a bowl to serve immediately.

Nutritional Value:

- Calories 211
- Total Fat 1 g
- Saturated Fat 0 g
- Cholesterol 0 mg
- Total Carbs 43.2 g
- Dietary Fiber 19.4 g
- Sugar 16.5 g
- Protein 7.6 g

Pita Sandwich

Preparation Time: 25 minutes
Cooking Time: 0 minutes
Servings: 4

Ingredients:

- 4 pita breads
- 8 tablespoons hummus
- 4 tablespoons pesto
- ½ cup cucumber, sliced and quartered
- 8 tablespoons feta cheese, crumbled
- 20 cherry tomatoes, halved
- ½ cup parsley, chopped
- 20 black olives, sliced

Method:

1. Heat pita breads in a pan and remove from the pan.
2. Spread hummus on the top of each pita and add pesto.
3. Layer with cherry tomatoes, black olives, parsley, feta cheese and cucumber.
4. Fold the bread tightly and cut in slices to serve.

Nutritional Value:

- Calories 469
- Total Fat 17.6 g
- Saturated Fat 5 g
- Cholesterol 20 mg
- Total Carbs 65.4 g
- Dietary Fiber 11.7 g
- Sugar 19 g
- Protein 17.7 g

Passata Cream Soup

Preparation Time: 40 minutes
Servings: 8

Ingredients:

- 2 celery sticks, finely chopped
- Shaved parmesan, chopped basil or pesto
- 2 small carrots, finely chopped
- 8 oz. soup pasta, cooked
- 1 onion, finely chopped
- 8 large ripe tomatoes
- 4 tablespoons cream
- 4 tablespoons olive oil
- 1 cup passata
- 1 vegetable stock

Method:

1. Heat oil in a saucepan on low heat and add onions, celery and carrots.
2. Sauté for about 8 minutes until soft and add the passata sauce and tomatoes.
3. Add water, vegetable stock, soup pasta and sugar and cook for about 20 minutes.
4. Stir in boiled pasta and cream with gentle stirring.
5. Garnish with parmesan, basil and pesto and serve warm.

Nutritional Value:

- Calories 237
- Total Fat 8.4 g
- Saturated Fat 1.3 g
- Cholesterol 1 mg
- Total Carbs 35 g
- Dietary Fiber 4.6 g
- Sugar 7.7 g
- Protein 6.2 g

Mediterranean Sardine Salad

Preparation Time: 20 minutes
Servings: 8

Ingredients:

- 4 (7 oz.) cans sardines in tomato sauce
- 1 cup black olives, roughly chopped
- 2 tablespoons red wine vinegar
- 6 oz. salad leaves
- 2 tablespoons olive oil
- 2 tablespoons caper, drained and diced

Method:

1. Divide the salad leaves into 8 plates and top with olives and capers.
2. Drain the sardines and reserve the sauce.
3. Slice the sardines roughly and divide equally between the plates.
4. Drizzle with tomato sauce, olive oil and vinegar to serve.

Nutritional Value:

- Calories 249
- Total Fat 17.1 g
- Saturated Fat 5 g
- Cholesterol 80 mg
- Total Carbs 5.7 g
- Dietary Fiber 2.1 g
- Sugar 2.1 g
- Protein 16.6 g

Chapter-8: Pizza and Snacks

Crispy Squid with Capers

Preparation Time: 25 minutes
Servings: 3

Ingredients:

- 1 garlic clove, crushed
- 2½ tablespoons mayonnaise
- Olive oil, for frying
- 3.5 oz. whole wheat flour
- 5 oz. baby squid, cleaned and sliced into thick rings
- 1 tablespoon caper, drained and finely chopped
- Lemon wedges, to serve

Method:

1. Combine together squid, capers and whole wheat flour in a bowl.
2. Heat oil in a skillet and deep fry capers and squids until golden.
3. Dish out the capers and squid in a plate.
4. Serve with mayonnaise, garlic and lemon wedges.

Nutritional Value:

- Calories 213
- Total Fat 5.1 g
- Saturated Fat 0.8 g
- Cholesterol 113 mg
- Total Carbs 29.9 g
- Dietary Fiber 1 g
- Sugar 0.9 g
- Protein 11 g

Goat's Cheese Pizza

Preparation Time: 55 minutes
Servings: 5

Ingredients:

- ½ handful black olives
- 1½ tablespoons pesto
- 3.5 oz. marinated grilled yellow and red bell peppers in olive oil
- 1/3 cup watercress
- ½ round focaccia loaf, halved
- 2 oz. soft goat's cheese, crumbled

Method:

1. Put the bell peppers in a colander to drain them and preserve their oil.
2. Top the loaf halves with a teaspoon of pesto over cut side.
3. Divide soft goat's cheese, watercress and bell pepper over each loaf half.
4. Mix the remaining pesto with 1 tablespoon bell pepper oil.
5. Drizzle this oil over the focaccia loafs and serve garnished with olives.

Nutritional Value:

- Calories 256
- Total Fat 12.2 g
- Saturated Fat 5.2 g
- Cholesterol 16 mg
- Total Carbs 28.7 g
- Dietary Fiber 2 g
- Sugar 2.5 g
- Protein 10.6 g

Spiced Tortilla

Preparation Time: 10 minutes
Servings: 6

Ingredients:

- 4 teaspoons curry spice
- 2 onions, sliced
- 2 pounds cooked potatoes, sliced
- 16 eggs, beaten
- 2 red chilies, deseeded and shredded
- 2 bunches coriander, finely chopped
- 2 tablespoons olive oil
- 3 cups cherry tomatoes

Method:

1. Heat oil in a skillet and add half of the red chilies and onions.
2. Sauté for about 5 minutes and add the curry spice, potatoes, coriander stalks and cherry tomatoes.
3. Whisk the eggs and pour into the pan.
4. Cook for about 10 minutes until it is set.
5. Preheat the grill and transfer the pan into the grill.
6. Grill for about 2 minutes and garnish with remaining red chilies and coriander leaves.
7. Dish out and slice to serve.

Nutritional Value:

- Calories 261
- Total Fat 12.5 g
- Saturated Fat 3.1 g
- Cholesterol 327 mg
- Total Carbs 24.3 g
- Dietary Fiber 3.5 g
- Sugar 2.8 g
- Protein 14.1 g

Mediterranean Artichoke Pizza

Preparation Time: 20 minutes
Servings: 12

Ingredients:

- 2 cups sun-dried tomato
- 2 cups pesto sauce
- 1 cup kalamata olives
- 8 ounces mozzarella cheese
- 2 cups artichoke heart
- 8 ounces feta cheese
- 2 pizza dough crusts
- 2 cups spinach leaves, wilted

Method:

1. Preheat the oven to 360 degrees F and grease lightly a baking pan.
2. Spread the pizza dough crust in the baking pan and stir in the pesto sauce.
3. Top with artichoke hearts, olives, spinach leaves and sun-dried tomatoes.
4. Sprinkle with feta cheese and transfer into the oven.
5. Bake for about 10 minutes and dish out to serve.

Nutritional Value:

- Calories 406
- Total Fat 14.1 g
- Saturated Fat 5 g
- Cholesterol 93 mg
- Total Carbs 41.3 g
- Dietary Fiber 5.6 g
- Sugar 4.3 g
- Protein 30 g

Stuffed Tomatoes

Preparation Time: 30 minutes
Servings: 3

Ingredients:

- 3 large tomatoes, heads chopped and seeds removed
- 1 mozzarella ball, sliced
- basil leaves, fresh
- 2 pieces red peppers, cooked
- 1 tablespoon red pesto

Method:

1. Preheat the oven to 380 degrees F and grease lightly a baking sheet.
2. Organize the tomatoes on a baking sheet with their cut side up.
3. Top the tomato bases with red peppers, mozzarella cheese and basil leaves.
4. Repeat the layers and top each base with a dollop of pesto.
5. Cover the tomato bases with their chopped off heads.
6. Transfer into the oven and bake for about 22 minutes.
7. Dish out in a platter and serve immediately.

Nutritional Value:

- Calories 280
- Total Fat 14.6 g
- Saturated Fat 4.2 g
- Cholesterol 13 mg
- Total Carbs 30.9 g
- Dietary Fiber 2.7 g
- Sugar 6.7 g
- Protein 8.5 g

Easy Tomato Pizzas

Preparation Time: 30 minutes
Servings: 8

Ingredients:

For the dough

- 3 cups warm water
- 2 sachets fast-action yeast
- 2 pounds bread flour, plus more to dust
- 4 tablespoons olive oil

For the topping

- 1 cup Parmesan cheese, grated
- 1 cup goat's cheese, grated
- 16 tomatoes, sliced
- 10 tablespoons roast tomato sauce

Method:

1. Preheat the oven to 400 degrees F and grease 4 baking sheets.
2. Mix yeast with flour in a bowl and stir in the water and olive oil.
3. Knead this dough well and cover the dough with a plastic sheet.
4. Keep it at a warm place for about 2 hours and knead the dough into sixteen equal balls.
5. Arrange these balls into 4 baking sheets and layer with roast tomato sauce, tomato slices, parmesan cheese, goat's cheese and seasoning.
6. Transfer in the oven and bake for about 15 minutes.
7. Dish out to serve and enjoy.

Nutritional Value:

- Calories 522
- Total Fat 8.6 g

- Saturated Fat 1.3 g
- Cholesterol 0 mg

- Total Carbs 97.1 g
- Dietary Fiber 6.3 g
- Sugar 7.6 g
- Protein 14.1 g

Herbed Olives

Preparation Time: 10 minutes
Servings: 12

Ingredients:

- ¼ teaspoon dried basil
- 6 cups olives
- 4 teaspoons extra-virgin olive oil
- Black pepper, to taste
- ¼ teaspoon dried oregano
- 2 garlic cloves, crushed

Method:

1. Mix together the olives with all other ingredients in a bowl.
2. Insert a toothpick into each olive and serve immediately.

Nutritional Value:

- Calories 93
- Total Fat 8.8 g
- Saturated Fat 1.2 g
- Cholesterol 0 mg
- Total Carbs 4.7 g
- Dietary Fiber 2.4 g
- Sugar 0 g
- Protein 0.7 g

Garlic Bread Pizzas

Preparation Time: 25 minutes
Servings: 8

Ingredients:

For the dough

- 2 pounds strong whole wheat flour, plus extra for rolling
- 4 tablespoons olive oil
- 2 sachets fast-action yeast
- 2 teaspoons salt

For the topping

- ½ cup almond butter, softened
- 2 teaspoons balsamic vinegar
- 2 tablespoons extra-virgin olive oil
- 4 garlic cloves, crushed
- 3 cups mozzarella, drained
- ½ cup basil leaves, roughly chopped
- 8 tomatoes, roughly chopped

Method:

1. Preheat the oven to 330 degrees F and grease 4 baking sheets.
2. Knead together all the ingredients for the dough in a bowl and roll out into 16 equal pieces.
3. Mix together garlic and butter in a bowl and pour over the dough.
4. Organize these pieces into the baking sheets and top with mozzarella cheese.
5. Transfer into the oven and bake for about 15 minutes.
6. Top with rest of the ingredients and immediately serve.

Nutritional Value:

- Calories 629
- Total Fat 21.8 g

- Saturated Fat 9.6 g
- Cholesterol 36 mg
- Total Carbs 92.2 g

- Dietary Fiber 4.6 g
- Sugar 3.6 g
- Protein 16 g

Chapter-9: Vegetarian

Charred Green Beans with Mustard

Preparation Time: 20 minutes
Servings: 2

Ingredients:

- 1 teaspoon whole-grain mustard
- 1/8 teaspoon salt
- 1/8 teaspoon black pepper
- 1½ tablespoons olive oil, divided
- ½ pound green beans, trimmed
- ½ tablespoon red-wine vinegar
- 1/8 cup toasted hazelnuts, chopped

Method:

1. Preheat a grill on high heat and grease a grill pan.
2. Mix green beans with ½ tablespoon of olive oil in a pan.
3. Transfer to the grill pan and grill the beans for about 8 minutes.
4. Mix the beans with mustard, olive oil, vinegar, salt and black pepper.
5. Top with hazelnuts and serve hot.

Nutritional Value:

- Calories 181
- Total Fat 14.6 g
- Saturated Fat 2.3 g
- Cholesterol 97 mg
- Total Carbs 8.5 g
- Dietary Fiber 6.1 g
- Sugar 2.4 g
- Protein 2.8 g

Lemony Mushroom and Herb Rice

Preparation Time: 20 minutes
Servings: 8

Ingredients:

- 4 large garlic cloves, finely chopped
- ¼ cup parsley, chopped
- 6 tablespoons chives, snipped
- 2½ cups chestnut mushrooms, diced
- 2 cups long grain rice
- 4 tablespoons olive oil
- 2 lemons, zested

Method:

1. Boil water with salt in a pan and add rice.
2. Cook for about 10 minutes while stirring continuously and drain them through a sieve.
3. Sauté mushrooms for about 5 minutes and stir in the garlic cloves.
4. Sauté for about 1 minute and toss in chives, parsley, lemon zest and drained rice.
5. Dish out to serve and enjoy.

Nutritional Value:

- Calories 281
- Total Fat 8.9 g
- Saturated Fat 1.4 g
- Cholesterol 0 mg
- Total Carbs 43.6 g
- Dietary Fiber 5.4 g
- Sugar 0.8 g
- Protein 9 g

Smoky Roasted Vegetables

Preparation Time: 1 hour 40 minutes
Servings: 4

Ingredients:

- ½ orange bell pepper, sliced
- 1 bay leaf
- 1 small red onion, sliced into rounds and separated
- ½ summer squash, cut into 3-inch sticks
- ½ teaspoon sea salt, divided
- 1/6 cup extra-virgin olive oil
- 2 small tomatoes, sliced
- ½ yellow bell pepper, sliced
- ½ zucchini, cut into 3-inch sticks
- 1 sprig fresh thyme
- ½ tablespoon balsamic vinegar
- ½ tablespoon red-wine vinegar
- ½ eggplant, cut into 3-inch sticks
- 2 sprigs fresh parsley
- 2 garlic cloves, divided

Method:

1. Preheat the oven to 360 degrees F and lightly grease a baking dish.
2. Season all the vegetables with salt and transfer to the baking dish.
3. Tie parsley, thyme and bay leaf with a kitchen string and place them at the center of the seasoned vegetables.
4. Drizzle with oil and top with garlic cloves.
5. Transfer in the oven and bake for about 1 hour 15 minutes.
6. Drizzle with vinegar and serve immediately.

Nutritional Value:

- Calories 231
- Total Fat 17.5 g

- Saturated Fat 2.5 g
- Cholesterol 0 mg
- Total Carbs 19.6 g

- Dietary Fiber 7.3 g
- Sugar 10.6 g
- Protein 3.6 g

Cashew and Bell Pepper Rice

Preparation Time: 15 minutes
Servings: 2

Ingredients:

- 2 oz. cashew nuts
- ½ yellow bell pepper, deseeded and finely sliced
- 1½ cups cooked basmati rice, cooled
- ½ green bell pepper, deseeded and finely sliced
- ½ small red onion, finely sliced

For the dressing

- ½ tablespoon brown sugar
- 1 tablespoon light soy sauce
- ¼ lemon, juiced
- 1½ tablespoons mango chutney
- 1 teaspoon curry powder
- ½ tablespoon oil

Method:

1. Mix together all the ingredients for dressing in a bowl.
2. Toast the cashews until golden brown and transfer to the mixed dressing.
3. Toss in rice, onions and bell peppers and immediately serve.

Nutritional Value:

- Calories 433
- Total Fat 17.1 g
- Saturated Fat 3.2 g
- Cholesterol 0 mg
- Total Carbs 70.6 g
- Dietary Fiber 2.5 g
- Sugar 14.1 g
- Protein 10.3 g

Roasted Vegetable Tabbouleh

Preparation Time: 35 minutes
Servings: 2

Ingredients:

- 1 (8-ounce) can garbanzo beans, rinsed and drained
- ¼ cup fresh parsley, chopped
- 2 small carrots, chopped
- 1/3 cup bulgur, boiled and drained
- ½ small red onion, chopped
- 1½ tablespoons lemon juice
- ¼ teaspoon black pepper
- ¼ teaspoon lemon peel, finely shredded
- 1 tablespoon water
- ½ medium tomatoes, chopped
- 1 tablespoon olive oil
- 1/8 teaspoon salt
- 1 teaspoon fresh thyme, snipped

Method:
1. Preheat the oven to 390 degrees F and lightly grease a baking dish.
2. Organize carrots and onions in a baking dish and drizzle with olive oil.
3. Bake for about 25 minutes and dish out in a bowl.
4. Add lemon peel, pepper, salt, bulgur, parsley, lemon juice and garbanzo to the baked veggies bowl and immediately serve.

Nutritional Value:
- Calories 370
- Total Fat 10.6 g
- Saturated Fat 1.5 g
- Cholesterol 0 mg
- Total Carbs 58.7 g
- Dietary Fiber 15.9 g
- Sugar 9.6 g
- Protein 14.1 g

Moroccan Couscous

Preparation Time: 20 minutes
Servings: 16

Ingredients:

- 2/3 cup dried apricots, chopped
- 2 oranges, juiced
- 2/3 cup golden raisins
- 1 teaspoon ground ginger
- 2 oranges, zested
- ½ teaspoon ground cinnamon
- 3 cups vegetable stock
- 2/3 cup dates, chopped
- 1 teaspoon ground cumin
- 4 cups whole-wheat couscous
- 1 cup slivered almonds, toasted
- ½ teaspoon coriander
- 2 tablespoons butter
- Salt, to taste
- 1 teaspoon turmeric
- ½ cup mint, chopped

Method:

1. Boil stock in a saucepan and add orange juice, zest, dates, apricots, raisins, couscous and spices.
2. Remove the pan from heat and allow the couscous to absorb the liquid for about 15 minutes.
3. Stir in the butter, mint and almonds and sprinkle with salt to serve.

Nutritional Value:

- Calories 264
- Total Fat 5 g
- Saturated Fat 1 g
- Cholesterol 4 mg

- Total Carbs 48 g
- Dietary Fiber 4 g
- Sugar 7.5 g
- Protein 8 g

Parmesan Roasted Broccoli

Preparation Time: 35 minutes
Servings: 8

Ingredients:

- 1 cup Parmesan cheese, grated
- 2 pounds broccoli florets, cut into bite-sized pieces
- 4 tablespoons olive oil
- 2 lemons, zested
- ¼ teaspoon sea salt
- Salt, to taste
- ¼ teaspoon red pepper flakes
- 4 tablespoons balsamic vinegar

Method:

1. Preheat the oven to 395 degrees F and lightly grease a baking sheet.
2. Season the broccoli florets with salt and place on the baking sheet.
3. Bake for about 15 minutes and top with parmesan cheese.
4. Bake these florets again for about 10 minutes and dish out in a bowl.
5. Season with lemon zest, salt, red pepper flakes and balsamic vinegar to serve.

Nutritional Value:

- Calories 146
- Total Fat 10.4 g
- Saturated Fat 3 g
- Cholesterol 10 mg
- Total Carbs 8.5 g
- Dietary Fiber 3 g
- Sugar 2.4 g
- Protein 7.7 g

Spinach Beans

Preparation Time: 30 minutes
Servings: 4

Ingredients:

- 2 cans (14½ ounces) diced tomatoes, undrained
- 2 cans (15 ounces) cannellini beans, rinsed and drained
- 4 garlic cloves, minced
- ½ teaspoon black pepper
- 28 ounces bacon, chopped
- 2 small onions, chopped
- ½ teaspoon salt
- 12 ounces fresh baby spinach
- 2 tablespoons olive oil
- 4 tablespoons Worcestershire sauce
- ¼ teaspoon red pepper flakes, crushed

Method:

1. Heat oil in a skillet on medium heat and add bacon.
2. Sauté until brown and stir in the garlic and onions.
3. Sauté for about 5 minutes and add Worcestershire sauce, seasonings and tomatoes.
4. Reduce the heat and cook for about 10 minutes.
5. Toss in the beans and spinach and cook for about 5 minutes.
6. Stir well and serve immediately.

Nutritional Value:

- Calories 475
- Total Fat 8.5 g
- Saturated Fat 1.2 g
- Cholesterol 0 mg
- Total Carbs 77.8 g
- Dietary Fiber 31.1 g
- Sugar 10.1 g
- Protein 28.2 g

Chapter-10: Seafood

Seafood with Couscous Salad

Preparation Time: 35 minutes
Servings: 8

Ingredients:

- 14 oz. cherry tomatoes
- 4 white fish fillets
- 2 small bunches basil, shredded
- 1 cucumber, diced
- 4 lemons, 2 zested and juiced and the other 2 cut into wedges
- 4 tablespoons balsamic vinegar
- 4 tablespoons pitted black olives, halved
- 2 red chilies, sliced
- 8 oz. couscous

Method:
1. Preheat the oven to 380 degrees F and lightly grease a baking sheet.
2. Arrange the fish on the baking sheet and add basil, sliced chilies and half of the lemon juice and zest.
3. Place the tomatoes on the edges of the fillets and transfer in the oven.
4. Bake for about 20 minutes and dish out.
5. Meanwhile, soak couscous in boiled water for about 18 minutes and drain well.
6. Mix together couscous, tomatoes, basil, cucumber, olives, lemon zest and juice in a bowl.
7. Serve the baked fish with the couscous salad and enjoy.

Nutritional Value:
- Calories 538
- Total Fat 13.3 g
- Saturated Fat 2.1 g
- Cholesterol 119 mg
- Total Carbs 56.8 g
- Dietary Fiber 6.4 g
- Sugar 5.5 g
- Protein 47.1 g

Sauce Dipped Mussels

Preparation Time: 20 minutes
Servings: 4

Ingredients:

- 2 green chilies, deseeded and chopped
- 2 shallots, finely diced
- 4 tablespoons olive oil
- 4 ripe tomatoes, soaked, drained and diced
- 2 garlic cloves, minced
- 2 glasses dry white wine
- 2 handfuls basil leaves
- 2 pounds mussels, cleaned
- 2 pinches sugar
- 2 teaspoons tomato paste
- Salt and black pepper, to taste

Method:
1. Heat olive oil in a skillet and stir in garlic, green chilies and shallots.
2. Sauté for about 3 minutes and add salt, black pepper, sugar, wine and tomatoes.
3. Cook for about 2 minutes and add mussels.
4. Cover with a lid and cook for about 5 minutes.
5. Garnish with basil leaves and immediately serve.

Nutritional Value:
- Calories 320
- Total Fat 17.8 g
- Saturated Fat 2.7 g
- Cholesterol 42 mg
- Total Carbs 19.4 g
- Dietary Fiber 2.4 g
- Sugar 6.8 g
- Protein 20.3 g

Lobster Rice Paella

Preparation Time: 40 minutes
Servings: 4

Ingredients:

- 4 garlic cloves, chopped
- 6 oz. French green beans
- Water, as required
- 2 small onions, chopped
- 1 teaspoon sweet Spanish paprika
- 3 tablespoons olive oil
- ½ cup fresh parsley, chopped
- 4 small lobster tails
- 2 large pinches of Spanish saffron threads soaked in ½ cup water
- 1 teaspoon cayenne pepper
- 2 large Roma tomatoes, finely chopped
- Salt, to taste
- 2 cups Spanish rice, soaked overnight and drained
- ½ teaspoon Aleppo pepper flakes
- 1-pound prawns, peeled and deveined

Method:

1. Boil lobster in water for about 2 minutes and transfer to an ice bath immediately.
2. Remove the meat from its shell and cut into small sized chunks.
3. Heat half of oil in a skillet and add onions.
4. Sauté for about 2 minutes and add rice.
5. Cook for about 3 minutes and add garlic and lobsters.
6. Season with paprika, saffron, salt and black pepper and add tomatoes and green beans.
7. Cover with a lid and lower the heat.
8. Cook for about 20 minutes and stir in shrimps.
9. Cover again and cook for about 14 more minutes.
10. Stir in parsley and lobster chunks to serve immediately.

Nutritional Value:

- Calories 464
- Total Fat 13.1 g
- Saturated Fat 2.2 g
- Cholesterol 239 mg

- Total Carbs 40.3 g
- Dietary Fiber 3.8 g
- Sugar 4.7 g
- Protein 30.4 g

Mixed Seafood Stew

Preparation Time: 20 minutes
Servings: 8

Ingredients:

- 2 tablespoons olive oil
- 2 teaspoons lemon peel, grated
- 2/3 cup white wine
- 2 medium onions, finely chopped
- 3 teaspoons garlic, minced and divided
- 1-pound plum tomatoes, seeded and diced
- ½ teaspoon red pepper flakes, crushed
- 2 tablespoons tomato paste
- 2 oz. red snapper fillets, cut into 1-inch cubes
- 2 pounds shrimps, peeled and deveined
- 2 cups clam juice
- 2/3 cup mayonnaise, reduced-fat
- Salt, to taste
- 1-pound sea scallops
- 2/3 cup fresh parsley, minced

Method:

1. Heat olive oil in a Dutch oven on medium heat and add garlic and onions.
2. Sauté for about 3 minutes and add tomatoes, lemon peel and pepper flakes.
3. Sauté for about 2 minutes and stir in wine, salt, tomato paste and clam juice.
4. Boil this mixture and reduce it to a simmer.
5. Cover the lid and cook for about 10 minutes.
6. Toss in the shrimps, scallops, parsley and red snapper fillets.
7. Cover and cook for 10 more minutes and serve topped with garlic and mayonnaise.

Nutritional Value:

- Calories 390

- Total Fat 15.3 g

- Saturated Fat 2.6 g
- Cholesterol 261 mg
- Total Carbs 20.1 g

- Dietary Fiber 1.9 g
- Sugar 7.3 g
- Protein 39 g

Seafood Garlic Couscous

Preparation Time: 30 minutes
Servings: 8

Ingredients:

- 8 scallions, sliced
- 4 (5.4-oz.) boxes garlic-flavored couscous, boiled and drained
- 1-pound raw shrimp, peeled, deveined and coarsely chopped
- 1 cup fresh parsley, chopped
- 4 tablespoons olive oil
- 2 pounds codfish, cut into 1-inch pieces
- 1 cup fresh chives, chopped
- Hot sauce, to taste
- 1-pound bay scallops
- Salt and black pepper, to taste

Method:

1. Mix shrimps, scallions, codfish, scallops, parsley, chives, salt and black pepper in a bowl.
2. Heat oil in a deep skillet and add the seafood mixture.
3. Sauté until golden and pour in the hot sauce.
4. Lower the heat and cover with a lid.
5. Divide the couscous into the serving plates and top evenly with the seafood mixture.
6. Dish out and serve immediately.

Nutritional Value:
- Calories 476
- Total Fat 9 g
- Saturated Fat 1.4 g
- Cholesterol 138 mg
- Total Carbs 68 g
- Dietary Fiber 4.9 g
- Sugar 0.8 g
- Protein 32.9 g

Fish and Vegetable Parcels

Preparation Time: 45 minutes
Servings: 4

Ingredients:

- 2 small lemon zests, finely grated
- 2½ cups baby potatoes, scrubbed
- 2 teaspoons olive oil
- 20 black olives
- 4 fresh rosemary sprigs
- 4 (6 oz.) firm haddock fillets
- 4 teaspoons sun-dried tomato paste
- 2 tablespoons capers, rinsed
- 4 teaspoons lemon juice

Method:

1. Preheat the oven to 325 degrees F and lightly grease 4 baking sheets.
2. Boil potatoes in a water mixed with salt in a large pot and transfer in a colander to drain well.
3. Place one fish fillet in each of the baking sheet and drizzle with lemon juice, tomato paste and lemon zest.
4. Arrange capers, potatoes and olives on the sides of haddock fillets and cover the fillets with rosemary sprigs.
5. Transfer in the oven and bake for about 30 minutes.
6. Dish out and serve immediately.

Nutritional Value:

- Calories 314
- Total Fat 16.5 g
- Saturated Fat 3.3 g
- Cholesterol 31 mg
- Total Carbs 29 g
- Dietary Fiber 3.8 g
- Sugar 2.7 g
- Protein 15.2 g

Saffron Fish Gratins

Preparation Time: 45 minutes
Servings: 6

Ingredients:

- 3 large garlic cloves, finely sliced
- 1 fennel bulb, trimmed and thinly sliced
- 2 (14 oz.) cans chopped tomatoes with herbs
- 1 large onion, thinly sliced
- ½ cup white wine
- 3 tablespoons olive oil
- 1 heaped teaspoon coriander seeds, lightly crushed
- 1 pinch saffron
- 2 pounds mixed skinless fish fillets, cut into chunks
- Green salad, to serve
- 1 bay leaf
- 1 bunch parsley, leaves roughly chopped
- ¼ cup panko breadcrumbs
- 1 tablespoon lemon juice
- ¼ cup parmesan cheese, finely grated
- 2 tablespoons tomato purée
- 1¾ cups raw king prawns, peeled

Method:

1. Preheat the oven to 385 degrees F and lightly grease a baking dish.
2. Heat oil in a large non-stick pan and add fennel, onions, garlic and coriander seeds.
3. Sauté for about 5 minutes and pour in saffron, wine, tomatoes, bay leaf and tomato puree.
4. Cook for about 15 minutes and add tomatoes mixture, prawns and fish chunks.
5. Cook for about 5 minutes and transfer the mixture in a baking dish.
6. Mix together parsley, breadcrumbs, parmesan cheese and black pepper and top it on the fish mixture.
7. Transfer in the oven and bake for about 20 minutes.

8. Dish out to serve warm.

Nutritional Value:

- Calories 501
- Total Fat 26.4 g
- Saturated Fat 5.5 g
- Cholesterol 52 mg

- Total Carbs 38.7 g
- Dietary Fiber 3.8 g
- Sugar 3.8 g
- Protein 27.5 g

Crusty Grilled Clams

Preparation Time: 15 minutes
Servings: 4

Ingredients:

- 4 tablespoons garlic and parsley butter
- 2 cups toasted bread crumbs
- Fresh herbs, to garnish
- 2 pounds clams, rinsed and debearded
- Chopped tomatoes, to garnish
- 2 lemons, zested

Method:

1. Boil clams in a water for about 3 minutes in a large pot.
2. Preheat the grill and lightly grease a baking sheet.
3. Mix zest and bread crumbs in a bowl.
4. Drizzle butter on top of the clams and place them shell side down on the baking sheet.
5. Top the bread crumbs mixture on the clams and transfer to the grill.
6. Cover the grill for about 4 minutes and let it cook.
7. Serve garnished with tomato and parsley.

Nutritional Value:

- Calories 510
- Total Fat 19.5 g
- Saturated Fat 8.9 g
- Cholesterol 94 mg
- Total Carbs 47.3 g
- Dietary Fiber 2.4 g
- Sugar 3.4 g
- Protein 34.3 g

Chapter-11: Poultry

Mediterranean Chicken with Potatoes

Preparation Time: 50 minutes
Servings: 3

Ingredients:

- 1/8 teaspoon dried thyme
- ½ teaspoon salt, divided
- 1-pound chicken breast, cut into bite-sized pieces
- 1 cup plum tomatoes, chopped
- 2 thyme sprigs
- 1/8 cup pitted kalamata olives, halved
- ¼ cup fresh parmesan cheese, grated
- ½ tablespoon olive oil
- 6 small red potatoes, halved
- 2 teaspoons garlic, minced and divided
- ¼ teaspoon black pepper, divided
- 1/3 cup dry white wine
- ¼ cup pepperoncini peppers, chopped
- ½ (14-ounce) can artichoke hearts, quartered
- ½ cup red onion, sliced
- 1/3 cup chicken broth
- 1 tablespoon fresh basil, chopped

Method:

1. Preheat the oven to 395 degrees F and lightly grease a baking sheet.
2. Mix together garlic, thyme, olive oil, potatoes, salt and black pepper in a bowl.
3. Transfer to a baking sheet and place in the oven.
4. Bake for about 30 minutes and dish out.
5. Grease a Dutch oven with cooking spray and warm it over medium heat.
6. Sprinkle the chicken with salt and black pepper.
7. Sear the seasoned chicken for 5 minutes per side.

8. Cook the chicken until soft and transfer into a plate.
9. Add onions to the same pan and stir in wine.
10. Cook the mixture until reduced to one-third.
11. Pour in broth along with chicken, potatoes, pepperoncini and olives.
12. Sauté for about 3 minutes and add tomatoes, salt, basil, garlic and artichokes.
13. Cook for another 3 minutes and garnish with thyme sprigs and parmesan cheese to serve.

Nutritional Value:

- Calories 534
- Total Fat 9.1 g
- Saturated Fat 2.6 g
- Cholesterol 88 mg
- Total Carbs 66.8 g
- Dietary Fiber 10.4 g
- Sugar 6.3 g
- Protein 43.8 g

Chicken with Tomato Sauce

Preparation Time: 25 minutes
Servings: 2

Ingredients:

- 1 (8-ounce) chicken breast, boneless and skinless, sliced into 4 equal sized pieces
- 1 tablespoon shallot, sliced
- ½ tablespoon garlic, minced
- 1/8 cup white whole-wheat flour
- ½ tablespoon fennel seeds, toasted and lightly crushed
- ¼ teaspoon salt, divided
- ¼ teaspoon black pepper, divided
- 1½ tablespoons olive oil, divided
- 1/8 cup balsamic vinegar
- ½ tablespoon butter
- ¼ cup cherry tomatoes, halved
- ½ cup low-sodium chicken broth

Method:

1. Season the chicken pieces with salt and black pepper.
2. Spread the flour in a dish and dredge the chicken in it.
3. Shake off the excess flour and keep aside.
4. Heat 1 tablespoon of olive oil in a large skillet and add chicken.
5. Sear for about 3 minutes on each side and transfer to a plate.
6. Cover with a foil and heat rest of the oil in the same pan.
7. Add shallots and tomatoes and cook for about 2 minutes until soft.
8. Pour in the vinegar and cook for about 1 minute.
9. Add broth, garlic, fennel seeds, salt and black pepper and cook for about 5 minutes.
10. Add butter and dish out to serve warm.

Nutritional Value:

- Calories 304
- Total Fat 19.2 g
- Saturated Fat 4.8 g
- Cholesterol 73 mg

- Total Carbs 9.4 g
- Dietary Fiber 1.7 g
- Sugar 1.1 g
- Protein 23.4 g

Roasted Mediterranean Chicken

Preparation Time: 55 minutes
Servings: 8

Ingredients:

- 2 teaspoons fresh rosemary, chopped
- 4 garlic cloves, minced
- 2 cups cherry tomatoes, diced
- 2 tablespoons fresh oregano
- 3 pounds chicken thighs, boneless and skinless
- 2 red onions, sliced
- 2 pounds asparagus spears, trimmed and cut
- 4 tablespoons balsamic vinegar
- 2 tablespoons fresh basil, chopped
- ½ teaspoon salt
- 16 oz. mushrooms, diced
- 2 tablespoons olive oil
- 20 pitted kalamata olives, sliced
- 4 tablespoons fresh parsley, chopped
- ½ teaspoon black pepper
- 1 cup green bell pepper, chopped
- 2 (16 ounces) cans cannellini beans

Method:

1. Preheat the oven to 435 degrees F and lightly grease a baking pan
2. Mix together rosemary, oregano, basil, salt, pepper and parsley in a bowl.
3. Place the chicken in the baking pan and season with herbs mixture.
4. Toss mushrooms with garlic, bell pepper, onions and olive oil.
5. Add this mixture to the baking pan around the chicken and transfer in the oven.
6. Roast for about 30 minutes and add asparagus, beans, tomatoes, olives, balsamic vinegar and basil mixture to the chicken pans.
7. Bake for about 15 minutes and dish out to serve warm.

Nutritional Value:

- Calories 498
- Total Fat 8.6 g
- Saturated Fat 0.6 g
- Cholesterol 109 mg

- Total Carbs 52.7 g
- Dietary Fiber 19.3 g
- Sugar 4.4 g
- Protein 56.1 g

Hasselback Caprese Chicken

Preparation Time: 35 minutes
Servings: 8

Ingredients:

- 6 ounces fresh mozzarella, halved and sliced
- 1 teaspoon salt, divided
- 4 chicken breasts, boneless and skinless
- 1 teaspoon black pepper, divided
- ½ cup prepared pesto
- 16 cups broccoli florets
- 2 medium tomatoes, sliced
- 4 tablespoons extra-virgin olive oil

Method:

1. Preheat the oven to 375 degrees F and lightly grease a baking sheet.
2. Sprinkle the chicken with salt and black pepper.
3. Stuff the mozzarella cheese and tomato slices in the chicken slits.
4. Brush with pesto and transfer the chicken breasts on the baking sheet.
5. Mix broccoli with olive oil, salt and black pepper in a large bowl.
6. Spread the broccoli mixture around the chicken and transfer in the oven.
7. Bake for about 25 minutes and dish out to serve warm.

Nutritional Value:

- Calories 309
- Total Fat 15.6 g
- Saturated Fat 4.6 g
- Cholesterol 101 mg
- Total Carbs 2.4 g
- Dietary Fiber 0.4 g
- Sugar 0.8 g
- Protein 38.9 g

Olive Chicken

Preparation Time: 45 minutes
Servings: 3

Ingredients:

- 2 garlic cloves, minced
- ¼ cup onions, diced
- 1 tablespoon white wine
- 1 teaspoon olive oil
- 3 chicken breast halves, skinless and boneless
- ¼ cup white wine
- 1 fennel bulb, sliced in half
- 1½ cups tomatoes, chopped
- 1 teaspoon fresh thyme, chopped
- 1/8 cup fresh parsley, chopped
- ½ tablespoon fresh basil, chopped
- Salt and black pepper, to taste
- ¼ cup kalamata olives

Method:

1. Heat oil with 2 tablespoons white wine in a large skillet on medium heat and add chicken.
2. Cook for about 6 minutes on each side and transfer the chicken to a plate.
3. Stir in garlic and onions and sauté for about 3 minutes.
4. Add fennel and tomatoes and allow it to boil.
5. Lower the heat and add rest of the white wine.
6. Cook for about 10 minutes and stir in the basil and thyme.
7. Cook for about 5 minutes and return the cooked chicken to the skillet.
8. Cover the cooking pan and cook on low heat.
9. Stir in olives and parsley and cook for about 1 minute.
10. Season with salt and black pepper to serve immediately.

Nutritional Value:

- Calories 428
- Total Fat 13.7 g
- Saturated Fat 4.4 g
- Cholesterol 173 mg

- Total Carbs 6.1 g
- Dietary Fiber 1.9 g
- Sugar 2.9 g
- Protein 67.9 g

Mediterranean Chicken and Orzo

Preparation Time: 2 hours 40 minutes
Servings: 8

Ingredients:

- 2 medium onions, halved and sliced
- 2 lemons, zested and juiced
- 1½ cups whole-wheat orzo
- 2 cups low-sodium chicken broth
- 2 pounds boneless, skinless chicken breasts, trimmed
- 4 medium tomatoes, chopped
- 1 teaspoon salt
- 4 tablespoons fresh parsley, chopped
- 1 teaspoon black pepper
- 2 teaspoons Herbs de Provence
- 2/3 cup black olives, quartered

Method:

1. Put chicken, lemon zest, juice, tomatoes, onion, broth, salt, black pepper and Herbs de Provence in a slow cooker.
2. Cover the lid and cook on High for about 2 hours.
3. Mix well and add orzo and olives to the dish.
4. Allow it to cook on High for about 30 more minutes.
5. Garnish with parsley and serve hot.

Nutritional Value:

- Calories 293
- Total Fat 10 g
- Saturated Fat 2.5 g
- Cholesterol 101 mg
- Total Carbs 15.1 g
- Dietary Fiber 2.6 g
- Sugar 3.2 g
- Protein 35.6 g

Lemon-Thyme Chicken

Preparation Time: 30 minutes
Servings: 8

Ingredients:

- ½ teaspoon black pepper
- 2 teaspoons crushed dried thyme, divided
- 8 small skinless, boneless chicken breast halves
- 2 lemons, thinly sliced
- 1 teaspoon salt
- 4 garlic cloves, minced
- 8 teaspoons extra-virgin olive oil, divided
- 2 pounds fingerling potatoes, halved lengthwise

Method:

1. Heat half of olive oil in a skillet over medium heat and add ½ teaspoon thyme, potatoes, salt and black pepper.
2. Cover and cook for about 12 minutes, while stirring occasionally.
3. Push the potatoes to a side and add rest of the olive oil and chicken.
4. Sear the chicken for about 5 minutes per side and season with thyme.
5. Arrange lemon slices over the chicken and cover the pan.
6. Cook for about 10 minutes and dish out to serve hot.

Nutritional Value:

- Calories 483
- Total Fat 9.4 g
- Saturated Fat 0.7 g
- Cholesterol 195 mg
- Total Carbs 18.8 g
- Dietary Fiber 2.1 g
- Sugar 1.2 g
- Protein 80.3 g

Mediterranean Chicken Quinoa Bowl

Preparation Time: 25 minutes
Servings: 8

Ingredients:

- ½ cup almonds, slivered
- 1/8 teaspoon black pepper
- 2 tablespoons extra-virgin olive oil, divided
- 1/8 teaspoon crushed red pepper
- 1 tablespoon fresh parsley, finely chopped
- 1 cup cooked quinoa
- 1/8 cup feta cheese, crumbled
- ½ teaspoon salt
- 1 small garlic clove, crushed
- ½ pound boneless, skinless chicken breasts, trimmed
- ½ (7-ounce) jar roasted red peppers, rinsed
- ½ teaspoon paprika
- 1/8 cup pitted Kalamata olives, chopped
- ½ cup cucumber, diced
- ¼ teaspoon ground cumin
- 1/8 cup red onions, finely chopped

Method:

1. Preheat the oven on broiler setting and lightly grease a baking sheet.
2. Sprinkle the chicken with salt and black pepper.
3. Transfer it on the baking sheet and broil for about 15 minutes.
4. Let the chicken cool for about 5 minutes and transfer to a cutting board.
5. Shred the chicken and keep aside.
6. Put almonds, paprika, black pepper, garlic, half of olive oil, red pepper and cumin in a blender.
7. Blend until smooth and dish out in a bowl.
8. Toss quinoa, red onions, 2 tablespoons oil, quinoa and olives in a bowl.

9. Divide the quinoa mixture in the serving bowls and top with cucumber, red pepper sauce and chicken.
10. Garnish with feta cheese and parsley to immediately serve.

Nutritional Value:

- Calories 741
- Total Fat 33.7 g
- Saturated Fat 6.7 g
- Cholesterol 109 mg
- Total Carbs 62.1 g
- Dietary Fiber 8.2 g
- Sugar 3.6 g
- Protein 48.4 g

Chapter-12: Meat

Lamb Pasta and Cheese

Preparation Time: 1 hour 50 minutes
Servings: 6

Ingredients:

- 1 pound lean lamb mince
- 14 oz. Penne pasta, boiled and drained
- Garlic bread, to serve
- 1 large onion, chopped
- 1 lamb stock cube
- ¼ cup parmesan cheese, grated
- 1 tablespoon olive oil
- 2 garlic cloves, crushed
- 2 (14 oz.) cans chopped tomatoes
- 1¼ cups ricotta
- 1 teaspoon ground cinnamon
- 1 tablespoon dried oregano
- ¼ cup milk

Method:

1. Preheat the oven to 380 degrees F and lightly grease a baking dish.
2. Heat olive oil in a medium skillet and add garlic and onions.
3. Sauté for about 3 minutes and add lamb mince.
4. Cook until brown and add oregano, cinnamon, stock cubes and tomatoes.
5. Cover this mixture and cook for about 10 minutes while occasionally stirring.
6. Mix parmesan cheese, milk and ricotta in a large bowl.
7. Add the macaroni and mix it with the cheese mixture.
8. Stir in the lamb sauce and top evenly with penne and cheese mixture.
9. Transfer the baking dish in the oven and bake for about 30 minutes.
10. Dish out to serve warm.

Nutritional Value:

- Calories 544
- Total Fat 21.4 g
- Saturated Fat 10.4 g
- Cholesterol 24 mg

- Total Carbs 57.9 g
- Dietary Fiber 3.7 g
- Sugar 4.6 g
- Protein 30.1 g

Mediterranean Beef Pinwheels

Preparation Time: 1 hour
Servings: 8

Ingredients:

- 4 tablespoons dried oregano leaves
- 2/3 cup lemon juice
- 4 pounds beef Flank Steak
- 4 tablespoons olive oil
- ½ cup low-fat feta cheese, crumbled
- 2 cups frozen spinach, chopped
- 2/3 cup olive tapenade
- 1 teaspoon salt
- 8 cups cherry tomatoes

Method:
1. Preheat the oven to 430 degrees F and lightly grease a baking dish.
2. Mix together oregano leaves, lemon juice, olive oil and salt in a bowl.
3. Place the beef Flank steak in a baking pan and pour this mixture over it.
4. Refrigerate the steak for about 3 hours to marinate well.
5. Remove the steak from the marinade and place on a cutting board.
6. Drizzle the steak with olive tapenade and top with feta cheese and spinach.
7. Roll the steak and tie with a kitchen string at different distances.
8. Slice the steak roll cross-sectionally into equal pieces and transfer into the baking dish.
9. Pour the remaining marinade over the slices and bake for about 35 minutes.
10. Dish out in a platter and serve warm.

Nutritional Value:
- Calories 243
- Total Fat 64.2 g
- Saturated Fat 4.9 g
- Cholesterol 90 mg
- Total Carbs 64.2 g
- Dietary Fiber 8.5 g
- Sugar 7.9 g
- Protein 27.5 g

Garlic and Rosemary Mediterranean Pork Roast

Preparation Time: 40 minutes
Servings: 12

Ingredients:

- 2 teaspoons salt
- 6 garlic cloves, sliced lengthwise into slivers
- 4 tablespoons olive oil
- 5 pounds pork sirloin roast
- 1 teaspoon black pepper
- 2 sprigs fresh rosemary

Method:

1. Preheat the oven to 260 degrees F and lightly grease a roasting pan.
2. Carve deep slits over the pork roasts with a sharp knife.
3. Stuff these slits with garlic slivers and rosemary.
4. Season with salt and black pepper and transfer into a skillet along with olive oil.
5. Cook until brown from both the sides and transfer into the roasting pan.
6. Place the roasting pan in the oven and bake for about 1 hour 10 minutes, flipping in between.
7. Dish out in a platter and immediately serve.

Nutritional Value:

- Calories 363
- Total Fat 18.7 g
- Saturated Fat 5.7 g
- Cholesterol 150 mg
- Total Carbs 0.6 g
- Dietary Fiber 0.1 g
- Sugar 0 g
- Protein 46.1 g

Vegetables Lamb Shanks

Preparation Time: 3 hours
Servings: 6

Ingredients:

For Spice Mix

- 2¼ teaspoons garlic powder
- ¾ teaspoon nutmeg, ground
- 1 teaspoon sweet Spanish paprika
- 1 teaspoon salt
- 1 teaspoon black pepper

For Lamb

- 2 celery ribs, chopped
- 2 cinnamon sticks
- 6 Lamb shanks
- 3 large carrots, peeled and diced
- 4 sprigs fresh thyme
- 2 tablespoons olive oil
- 1-pound baby potatoes, scrubbed
- 3 cups low-sodium beef broth
- 2 sprigs fresh rosemary
- 1 medium yellow onion, roughly chopped
- 2 cups dry red wine
- 1 (28-oz) can peeled tomatoes

Method:

1. Preheat the oven to 360 degrees F.
2. Mix together all the spices in a bowl and rub this mixture over the lamb.
3. Heat half of olive oil in a Dutch oven on medium-high heat and add the shanks.

4. Sear for about 10 minutes on each side and add carrots, onions, celery and potatoes.
5. Sauté for about 8 minutes and stir in the red wine.
6. Add cinnamon, tomatoes, thyme, rosemary and broth and turn off the heat after 10 minutes.
7. Place the covered Dutch oven in the oven and bake for about 2 hours 30 minutes.
8. Dish out in a platter and serve warm.

Nutritional Value:

- Calories 369
- Total Fat 18.9 g
- Saturated Fat 5 g
- Cholesterol 135 mg
- Total Carbs 1.7 g
- Dietary Fiber 0.6 g
- Sugar 0.2 g
- Protein 46.2 g

Mediterranean Beef Kofta

Preparation Time: 30 minutes
Servings: 8

Ingredients:

- 1 cup onions, minced
- 2 tablespoons olive oil
- 2 pounds ground beef

Spices

- 1 teaspoon salt
- ½ teaspoon dried mint leaves
- ½ teaspoon allspice
- 1 teaspoon ground coriander
- ½ teaspoon ground cinnamon
- 1 teaspoon ground cumin

Method:

1. Mix together ground beef, olive oil, onions, spices and mint leaves in a large bowl.
2. Shape beef kebabs on the wooden skewers with this mixture.
3. Refrigerate these beef kebabs for about 20 minutes.
4. Preheat the grill and grill these kebabs for about 15 minutes while constantly flipping.
5. Remove from the grill and serve warm.

Nutritional Value:

- Calories 216
- Total Fat 12.2 g
- Saturated Fat 4 g
- Cholesterol 84 mg
- Total Carbs 1.3 g
- Dietary Fiber 0.2 g
- Sugar 0.3 g
- Protein 26.1 g

Blue Cheese-Topped Pork Chops

Preparation Time: 25 minutes
Servings: 8

Ingredients:

- 4 tablespoons fat-free Italian salad dressing
- ½ cup reduced-fat blue cheese, crumbled
- 2 pinches cayenne pepper
- 8 (6-ounce) bone-in pork loin chops
- 2 tablespoons fresh rosemary, snipped

Method:

1. Preheat the oven at broiler settings and line a broiler tray with a foil sheet.
2. Mix the Italian salad dressing with cayenne pepper.
3. Brush the dressing mixture on both sides of the pork chops.
4. Place the pork chops on the broiler tray and broil the pork chops for about 10 minutes, flipping in between.
5. Top the chops with blue cheese and rosemary to serve.

Nutritional Value:

- Calories 506
- Total Fat 21.6 g
- Saturated Fat 3.7 g
- Cholesterol 193 mg
- Total Carbs 3.3 g
- Dietary Fiber 0.9 g
- Sugar 1.6 g
- Protein 70.8 g

Baked Lamb Tray

Preparation Time: 55 minutes
Servings: 8

Ingredients:

- 4 onions, halved
- ½ cup feta cheese, crumbled
- 2½ cups lamb mince
- 4 large potatoes, cut into wedges
- 24 cherry tomatoes
- ½ cup fresh white breadcrumbs
- 2 large handfuls mint, chopped
- 4 tablespoons olive oil
- 2 eggs, beaten
- 4 zucchinis, cut into batons
- Salt and black pepper, to taste

Method:

1. Preheat the oven to 360 degrees F and lightly grease a roasting pan.
2. Mix the lamb mince, breadcrumbs, eggs, onions and mint in a bowl.
3. Make small patties out of this mixture and place in a roasting pan.
4. Arrange the potatoes, onion wedges, zucchinis and tomatoes in the pan.
5. Drizzle the patties with olive oil and season with salt and and black pepper.
6. Transfer in the oven and bake for about 40 minutes.
7. Garnish these patties with remaining feta cheese and mint to serve.

Nutritional Value:

- Calories 599
- Total Fat 28.3 g
- Saturated Fat 9.9 g
- Cholesterol 132 mg
- Total Carbs 57.1 g
- Dietary Fiber 11.4 g
- Sugar 16.7 g
- Protein 32.8 g

Greek Beef Steak and Hummus Plate

Preparation Time: 25 minutes
Servings: 8

Ingredients:

- 2 tablespoons plus 2 teaspoons garlic, minced
- 2 cups hummus
- ½ cup fresh oregano leaves, chopped
- 2 medium cucumbers, thinly sliced
- ½ teaspoon black pepper
- 2 pounds beef sirloin steaks, boneless, cut 1 inch thick
- 2 teaspoons black pepper
- 4 tablespoons Romesco Sauce
- 2 tablespoons lemon peel, grated
- 6 tablespoons fresh lemon juice

Method:
1. Preheat a grill on medium heat and lightly grease a grill grate.
2. Mix together all the dry spices and rub on both sides of the beef steaks.
3. Grill the steaks for about 15 minutes.
4. Mix together sliced cucumber, lemon juice and black pepper in a bowl.
5. Slice the grilled steak and sprinkle with salt and black pepper.
6. Serve with Romesco sauce, hummus and cucumber strips.

Nutritional Value:
- Calories 463
- Total Fat 37.7 g
- Saturated Fat 7.6 g
- Cholesterol 28 mg
- Total Carbs 68.7 g
- Dietary Fiber 14.5 g
- Sugar 19.7 g
- Protein 36.4 g

Chapter-13: Desserts

Compote Dipped Berries Mix

Preparation Time: 20 minutes
Servings: 8

Ingredients:

- 2 cups fresh strawberries, hulled and halved lengthwise
- 4 sprigs fresh mint
- 2 cups fresh blackberries
- 1 cup pomegranate juice
- 2 teaspoons vanilla
- 6 orange pekoe tea bags
- 2 cups fresh red raspberries
- 1 cup water
- 2 cups fresh golden raspberries
- 2 cups fresh sweet cherries, pitted and halved
- 2 cups fresh blueberries
- 2 ml bottle Sauvignon Blanc

Method:

1. Preheat the oven to 290 degrees F and lightly grease a baking dish.
2. Soak mint sprigs and tea bags in boiled water for about 10 minutes in a covered bowl.
3. Mix together all the berries and cherries in another bowl and keep aside.
4. Cook wine with pomegranate juice in a saucepan and add strained tea liquid.
5. Toss in the mixed berries to serve and enjoy.

Nutritional Value:

- Calories 356
- Total Fat 0.8 g
- Saturated Fat 0.1 g
- Cholesterol 0 mg
- Total Carbs 89.9 g
- Dietary Fiber 9.4 g

- Sugar 70.8 g

- Protein 2.2 g

Fruity Almond Cake

Preparation Time: 2 hours 10 minutes
Servings: 4

Ingredients:

- ¾ cup butter, softened
- 2½ oz. whole almond
- 1 large orange, zested and juiced
- 2½ oz. whole wheat flour
- 1 teaspoon mixed spice
- 1-pound mixed dried fruit
- ¾ cup light muscovado sugar
- ½ vanilla pod, seeds scraped
- 2 large eggs, beaten
- ¼ cup sherry
- 2 oz. ground almond

Method:

1. Preheat the oven to 300 degrees F and lightly grease a cake pan with butter.
2. Mix sherry, fruits, orange juice and zest in a bowl and refrigerate overnight.
3. Beat sugar and vanilla seeds in butter until creamy and smooth.
4. Combine mixed spice, whole wheat flour and ground almond until smooth.
5. Add in the marinated fruits and whole almonds.
6. Pour the batter in the baking dish and transfer in the oven.
7. Bake for about 1 hour 30 minutes and dish out.
8. Reduce the heat of the oven to 270 degrees F and bake for 20 more minutes to enjoy.

Nutritional Value:

- Calories 613
- Total Fat 41.8 g
- Saturated Fat 19.8 g
- Cholesterol 169 mg
- Total Carbs 54.1 g
- Dietary Fiber 2.7 g

- Sugar 36.8 g

- Protein 9 g

Orange Sesame Cookies

Preparation Time: 35 minutes
Servings: 12

Ingredients:

- ½ lemon, juiced1 cup brown sugar
- 1 cup extra virgin olive oil
- ½ cup orange juice, freshly squeezed
- ½ teaspoon ground cloves
- ½ cup sesame seed
- 3¾ cups whole wheat flour
- ½ shot brandy
- 1 teaspoon baking soda
- ½ teaspoon ground cinnamon

Method:

1. Preheat the oven to 360 degrees F and lightly grease a baking tray.
2. Beat sugar with olive oil until dissolved and add orange juice.
3. Beat again for about 2 minutes and stir in lemon juice, cinnamon, cloves, baking soda and brandy.
4. Fold in the whole wheat flour and mix well to prepare smooth cookie dough.
5. Make small cookies out of this mixture and roll in the sesame seeds.
6. Arrange the cookies on the baking tray and transfer in the oven.
7. Bake for about 25 minutes and dish out to serve and enjoy.

Nutritional Value:

- Calories 375
- Total Fat 20.2 g
- Saturated Fat 2.9 g
- Cholesterol 0 mg
- Total Carbs 44.5 g
- Dietary Fiber 1.9 g
- Sugar 12.8 g
- Protein 5.2 g

Popped Quinoa Bars

Preparation Time: 10 minutes
Servings: 3

Ingredients:

- 2 (4 oz.) semi-sweet chocolate bars, chopped
- ½ tablespoon peanut butter
- ½ cup dry quinoa
- ¼ teaspoon vanilla

Method:

1. Toast dry quinoa in a pan until golden and stir in chocolate, vanilla and peanut butter.
2. Spread this mixture in a baking sheet evenly and refrigerate for about 4 hours.
3. Break it into small pieces and serve chilled.

Nutritional Value:

- Calories 278
- Total Fat 11.8 g
- Saturated Fat 6.6 g
- Cholesterol 7 mg
- Total Carbs 36.2 g
- Dietary Fiber 3.1 g
- Sugar 15.4 g
- Protein 6.9 g

Greek Baklava

Preparation Time: 1 hour 10 minutes
Servings: 12

Ingredients:

- 2 cups walnuts, chopped
- 1 teaspoon ground cloves
- 1 cup sesame seeds
- 3 tablespoons honey
- 2 cups almonds, chopped
- 12 sheets phyllo pastry dough
- 1 cup extra-virgin olive oil
- 2 teaspoons ground cinnamonSyrup:
- 2½ cups honey
- 2 lemons, peeled and juiced
- 4 cups water
- 2 cinnamon sticks

Method:

1. Preheat the oven to 360 degrees F and lightly grease a baking sheet and phyllo sheets with olive oil.
2. Mix together almonds, cinnamon, walnuts, sesame seeds, cloves and honey in a bowl.
3. Place this layer in the baking dish and top with 3 more layers of phyllo sheets.
4. Pour in half of the nut mixture and evenly spread it.
5. Add layers of 4 oiled phyllo sheets again and top with the other half of the nut mixture.
6. Transfer in the oven and bake the baklawa for about 35 minutes.
7. Slice the layers into squares and allow it to cool.
8. Meanwhile, let simmer all the sauce ingredients for about 15 minutes.
9. Pour it over the baklava pieces and serve immediately.

Nutritional Value:

- Calories 651
- Total Fat 43.8 g
- Saturated Fat 4.5 g
- Cholesterol 0 mg

- Total Carbs 61.3 g
- Dietary Fiber 5.6 g
- Sugar 40.1 g
- Protein 13 g

Honey Yogurt Cheesecake

Preparation Time: 1 hour 10 minutes
Servings: 8

Ingredients:

- 1 cup Greek yogurt
- Fresh fruit, to serve
- 3 tablespoons almond butter, melted
- 1 cup honey
- 3 tablespoons almonds, flaked
- 2 eggs
- 2 tablespoons bread crumbs
- 1 orange, zested
- 4 oz. amaretti biscuits
- 26 oz. mascarpone
- 1 lemon, zested

Method:

1. Preheat the oven to 290 degrees F and lightly grease a baking dish.
2. Seal biscuits and almonds in a ziplock bag and crush with a rolling pin.
3. Toss this mixture with almond butter and bread crumbs and transfer evenly into a baking dish.
4. Bake for about 10 minutes and dish out.
5. Whisk eggs, yogurt and mascarpone with a beater and stir in honey, orange and lemon zest.
6. Transfer the batter to the baked crust and cover the pan with a foil tent.
7. Bake for about 1 hour and garnish with honey and almonds to serve.

Nutritional Value:

- Calories 368
- Total Fat 30 g
- Saturated Fat 11 g
- Cholesterol 217 mg
- Total Carbs 10 g
- Dietary Fiber 8 g

- Sugar 0.3 g
- Protein 17 g

Almond Orange Pandoro

Preparation Time: 10 minutes
Servings: 12

Ingredients:

- 2 large oranges, zested
- 2½ cups mascarpone
- ½ cup almonds, whole
- 2½ cups coconut cream
- ½ pandoro, diced
- 2 tablespoons sherry

Method:

1. Whisk cream with mascarpone, icing sugar, ¾ zest and half sherry in a bowl.
2. Dice the pandoro into equal sized horizontal slices.
3. Place the bottom slice in a plate and top with the remaining sherry.
4. Spoon the mascarpone mixture over the slice.
5. Top with almonds and place another pandoro slice over.
6. Continue adding layers of pandoro slices and cream mixture.
7. Dish out to serve.

Nutritional Value:

- Calories 346
- Total Fat 10.4 g
- Saturated Fat 3 g
- Cholesterol 10 mg
- Total Carbs 8.5 g
- Dietary Fiber 3 g
- Sugar 2.4 g
- Protein 7.7 g

Honey Glazed Pears

Preparation Time: 35 minutes
Servings: 3

Ingredients:

- 2 tablespoons almond butter
- 3 ripe medium pears, peeled, halved and cored
- 1 teaspoon orange zest
- 1/3 cup salted pistachios, roasted and chopped
- ¼ cup pear nectar
- Dollop of cream
- 3 tablespoons honey
- ½ cup mascarpone cheese

Method:

1. Preheat the oven to 400 degrees F and lightly grease a baking pan.
2. Spread the sliced pears in a baking pan with their cut sides down.
3. Top with butter, honey, nectar and orange zest.
4. Transfer in the oven and roast these pears for about 25 minutes.
5. Mix sugar with mascarpone and pour on the baked pears.
6. Garnish with honey and pistachios to serve.

Nutritional Value:

- Calories 349
- Total Fat 14.3 g
- Saturated Fat 8.4 g
- Cholesterol 41 mg
- Total Carbs 53.6 g
- Dietary Fiber 5.8 g
- Sugar 41.5 g
- Protein 6 g

Conclusion

With the right approach and understanding of the meal prepping any diet can be adapted to its best. And it sure makes it easier for all the Mediterranean diet followers. Mere understanding of a diet cannot guarantee an effective formula for its adoption. It needs a complementary design or a plan which make it all happen. That is where the meal prepping comes in and ensures efficiency. Each recipe in this cookbook is created with the objective to provide a healthy, and quickly made a meal at home. With a variety of sections touching all the food genres, we have unlocked all the levels of a complete Mediterranean diet. Classified into separate chapters, this book has elaborately unfolded the entire science behind the Mediterranean diet and meal prepping. If you are caught with the brilliance of these approaches, then it is a must read for you all. Learn and then have experience of both the good flavors and flourishing health. Say no to bad fats and toxic food, bring delightful ingredients into better use.

CPSIA information can be obtained
at www.ICGtesting.com
Printed in the USA
LVHW100806021120
670426LV00010B/365